# Oh, Look!

# My Blue Period.

### E. J. Ginger

Oh, Look! My Blue Period.

979-8-9941023-0-5

# Disclaimer & Trigger Warning

This chapbook is not a work of fiction. Every emotion written has been an emotion felt by the author. The content of this chapbook contains descriptions or implications of the following:

Suicidal ideation

Grief

Infant Death

Stillbirth

Depression

Anxiety

Dissociation

*To those who have held me close during my darkest days, and to all the other souls lost in their own blue periods.*

*But most importantly to my children:*

*Josephine, Kenton, and Angel.*

*I love you.*

*I miss you.*

# Contents

VI

# A Swan's Song

Who I was is not who I am.
I have doubts she ever existed.
I have reminders, of course:
flashbacks like a movie trailer, picturesque scenes
of a life loved but never lived.
Or a play; humorous and horrible.
Each phase of my life corresponding to an Act,
punctuated and timed by the calamities of every
scene, and sparsely freckled like ink splotches with
blessings as the Playwright pens my life.

# Anxiety

# A Peak Inside My Mind

Anxiety riddled, writing anxiety riddles—
cute little rhyming schemes.
Bursting at the seams—
wondering—
when did I last relax?
What does that even mean?
The definition is lost somewhere between age seven
wondering what's for dinner and age nineteen
wondering if I'll have a dinner.


The monsters plague my mind—
demons shred the last scraps of my sanity.
I try… I fight…
I'm suffocating in all this lucidity.
It's easier to just let the burdens take me—
Do you know what it's like to have a minefield of a
mindfield?
One mis-step—one mis-thought—
and the world shatters around you.
White pain—white noise—
exploding thoughts—exploding bombs—
ripping apart your body—tearing apart your soul—
fragmented like the shards of a broken mirror.


…was I ever really whole?

# Escapism

Have you read this book?
I've got the whole trilogy.
It's beautiful. I think I have a new favorite author.
It's way better than me staring at the wall lost in thought.
Books get expensive, though…

Hey, I fell down a video rabbit hole yesterday;
spent a few too many hours learning about radicals
and kana and pitch accents for Japanese.
I was almost late to work.
Hmm? Oh, yeah, I was kind of worried, but not
really at the same time.
I turned on my audiobook for the commute so I
didn't have to think about it.
Oh! Unrelated note, have you watched that season
finale?
I cried.
No, I haven't thought about how emotional I am
lately. I mean, yeah, I know why, but…

Did you hear Taylor Swift's newest single yet?
I've had it on repeat. It's wonderful. The whole
album is poetry.
Like Shakespeare.
Ooh! Shakespeare!
Let me tell you my favorite soliloquies.

I can recite them for you if you want today, and tomorrow, and tomorrow, and tomorrow, and all the tomorrows after those!

Sorry. I'm a bit much right now.

I'm trying not to think about my anxiety (it makes me anxious).

And I've been learning all I can about neo-paganism and witchiness and good vibes and manifesting things for yourself—just speak it enough times and believe!

Though, I haven't given a lot of thought as to what I want to manifest…

I'll worry about it later.

I finally downloaded my Kindle app and now I can download free books to read whenever.

I can't afford the Kindle unlimited or purchasing any of the books right now, but that's another thing to worry about later.

The weather patterns have been weird—well, not weird, more typical Midwest season transition weather, but it got me sick all the same.

I had to call off work, but it's all right!

I sick-binged a new show and stuffed my face with pizza.

Yeah, I've been sad.

It's kind of hard to be anything else most days.

It's kind of hard to do anything most days.

No. I don't want to talk about it.

Anyway. What's going on with you?

# Depression

# Out of the Woodwork

It comes to me in the cold and dark and quiet like a shadow. But it's cold and dark and quiet so I never see it until it's upon me. It doesn't speak. It doesn't even breathe, but it has life enough to wrap itself around me, bury itself in me, and remind me of its presence at every moment. Sometimes it disappears. For minutes, hours, weeks. Always to return.

It comes to me in the warmth and light and sound. But it's fast so I never see it until it's upon me, and the smile drops from my face, the laughter falls on deaf ears. It evaporates the warmth from my soul like the harshest brumal wind. It makes the most colorful days gray and dull. Any joyful fire is smothered before it can spark. And any sorrow is given space to flare. Sometimes it disappears. For minutes, hours, weeks. Always to return.

## My Lonely Bed

My bed's call is like that of a lonely lover.

Except she's not lonely because I rarely leave her.
She's perfect and warm and safe.
There's an ache in my heart and a hollow space in
my gut where winter winds viciously swirl, and
I know it's me craving to return to her.

It's me wishing I wasn't at this bar.
It's me wishing I hadn't felt so guilty as to say yes
to leaving her.
And it's me wanting my pen and paper to scratch
out my desperation
because heaven and hell forbid I'm able to vocalize
how I feel.
I write these words—my blood for ink; this razor, a
pen.
I write these words.
Chicken scratch scrawl on pale paper, on pale skin.
And I want to tell you. Except that I don't.

Because I'm not depressed.
There's a roof over my head.
It protects me from the harsh cold and wind. It hides
me when all I want is to disappear into it.
I have food in my stomach. . .when I feel like
eating.

There are arms that hold me at request;
voices that whisper adoration and love, and I hear
them.
I believe them, but I don't tell them so.


Emotions terrify me.
Socialization paralyzes me.
The thought of sitting in silence because what am I
supposed to say to these people;
my friends, my family.
No words sound right as they perch on the tip of my
tongue.
Do I just smile? A laugh that sounds sincere?


I motion through it, dreaming on when I can return
to my room, crawl into my bed, and remind her that
she is mine


and I am hers.

# A Daedalus Design

Are those lights real?
They line the path and guide me,
so they must not be.
Nothing's ever that easy.
Unless it's not the exit they lead to.
Which way was I going?
Yes, I've read this book before;
know the story too well.
All tunnels look the same:
lamps along the walls with whipping shadows that
mimic the flicker of flames.
They all bring me back here or there or somewhere
like it.
They're all the same.
I should know better anyway.
I've never escaped my mind before.

# Adjusting to Midnight

I did not adopt the dark;
never beckoned it close.
I was chosen.
It arrived and plucked me from the sunlight and
embraced me in arms of moonbeams and starlight;
it sang to me in owl songs, in the howls of wolves.
Never will I belong anywhere else anymore than
here.

# Grief

# Nobody Wants to Hear That

"Do you have children?"

It's a regular question I hear. It's asked when I interview for a job, when I meet someone new, when I complain of my exhaustion.

But I never know how to answer. Saying "no" sounds like a lie, but so does "yes". And if I say "yes" then—

"How many?"

"How old?"

And then what?

A daughter and a son, but my daughter was stillborn, and my son was three months premature. He was five days old when he—

But nobody wants to hear that.

So, I tell them "no" and swallow the painful wrongness of the word and shove aside the images of a tiny boy, one pound big, in his incubator under the blue light; of a tinier girl, wrapped in a blanket too small to even be a washcloth.

I tell them "no", and beneath my straight face I ache with fury and grief.

"Well, why are you so tired?"

What can I say?

I don't deal with my emotions well so I procrastinate them, and my grief developed into a depression I can't escape. My meds don't help. I just started them. They make me sleepier.

Every time I close my eyes I see a pair of baby blue ones staring back at me or I dream of a giggle I never heard.

Maybe I mention how I long for sleep, but fear my dreams. Because while my life feels like one tragedy after another, my dreams are a blissful torture that only hurts after I wake.

My anxiety causes my heart to race and my adrenaline to spike. I believe the stress is killing me. Each breath I take is filled with dread and worry; a poisonous gnawing at my gut and chest every day.

Depression, anxiety, stress—among many things, they cause fatigue.

I don't even think my body knows how to relax at this point. Shoulders hunched, jaw clenched. Every muscle tensed to perfection, awaiting the next disaster to strike.

But…nobody wants to hear that.

So, I sigh and grimace. "I have a new puppy—"

She's two years old already and sleeps very well at night.

"—that thinks it's playtime all the time."

They laugh or nod in agreement or share their own woes of puppy parenthood.

And the moment is gone, and I am the only one who remembers the original question. And when everybody goes home, lays in their warm beds to sleep, I stare at the ceiling—the wall—the inside of my eyelids—and try not to think.

But nobody wants to hear that.

# The Things I Hold Dear

The pale pink carnations at Mary's feet and the
silent snowdrops I've cried.
The hugs you never got and the love I carry inside.
Mums wet with rain, snow, and tears.
The sunshine on my face. A smile I never saw.
The wisps of your hair, strawberry blonde on your
head.
Your kicks and your punches that you never pulled.
The blue I bet was in your eyes, the ones that never
met mine.
A book of love and songs of joy.
Tales of faeries and dragons and phoenixes,
adventures for a little boy.
A dear friend's laugh, their curses, and strength.
Their support when there was nothing more I could
take.
The coffee I shouldn't have and the light of the
stars.
The smell of autumn and the crunch of snow under
my foot.
Halloween and all its glory.
And the New Year and the hope it brings.
And this I confess last for to think on it brings me to
tears:

Those 26 weeks I had always with you.

These are but a few things I hold dear.

# For My Birthday

There's hundreds of things I could ask for.
A new book or twenty,
a paid off car or house,
chocolates or flowers or a pretty notebook for my
musings;
but while sweet and lovely,
these gifts do not compare to my heart's desire.
If I could have one gift, if I could have three gifts,
it would be to see my children whole and happy and
alive;
to know their love and laughter, to hold them
through their sorrows,
to guide them through hurdles and celebrate their
successes.
To see my children whole and happy and alive.

# A Flickering

It's the first week of September, and I wish you
were here.
The weather is already changing. Autumn is almost
here.
I've tried to explain
my love for this season and my disdain.
I used to hate the cold;
how it stings and how it bites.
But now the chill
resonates with something inside;
like a lack of warmth
meets a lack of…life.

# Broken like Me

I threw the tissue box across the room.

It smacked against the wall, rebounded and landed on the floor. Immediately, I wished for something heavier, more fragile. I wanted something that would break like I was broken.

This unnamed thing and myself shattering. Our shards scattered across the floor to go missing. Because once again—*once again*—there are now parts of me that will never be found.

It was a day like any other, overflowing with the anxiety and stress of what I will learn. Good news was good. No news was bad. Bad news had been both.

I never was, and still am not, sure how to explain the rage and relief I felt in equal measure at that moment; the numbness in my body not caused by the chill of the ultrasound room. The blunt force trauma against my heart from my expectations having been met and my disbelief for the same reason.

Angel was our third and our last. Their older brother's and sister's spirits hold them close; close like I wish to, but I won't because I can't.

Instead I sit quietly in the dimly lit room. My silence is loud, and the darkness around it louder.

Anger

# Blasphemous

Dear, God—
Wait, stop. That's not right.
Hey, fucker—
No. Not like that either.


Give me a second. Sorry. Sometimes my mouth
gives voice to my thoughts before they're in the
proper order. Let's try that again.


Josephine Lorraine.
Kenton Carl III.
Angel Lee.


Do they sound familiar?
Oh. Sorry, Buddy, I wasn't talking to just You.
See, there's pantheons, and You all have something
to answer to.


The universe's deities best be prepared. You best
kneel and scrape and grovel for my forgiveness.
For my mind is sharp and full of terror, and my
words are a lash that will flay You to shreds.

True, my countenance is calm, my smile easy, but it's all artificial—maybe like Your intelligence.


You see, I am a placid Lake, bubbling under the surface, ready to break and ripple at the smallest pebble.
Maybe someday I'll write pretty words in a Cottage of pretty birds, but today I'd scream at them with anguish they've never heard.


Away, they'd fly.


Because what are my words worth to them?
Worthless, yes, but worthwhile while I have the attention, the attraction, the absolute adoration of—


Sorry. I remembered that I never got to my question. My brain train gets derailed like that sometimes. Give me a moment while I reorganize my mind.


Ah, yes. There it is.
If free will is truly free then what happened to my will to live?
I never got my final past due notice, but it's been repossessed all the same.
Repossessed like I've been repossessed by the depression and obsession—

obsession in that I'm obsessed with being depressed
because if I'm not this angry traumatized
blasphemer, who am I?
Who am I?


How many Emilys are there?
How many writers who can't seem to write?
How many motherless children—
No, wait, sorry—
How many childrenless mothers—
No, wait, sorry—
If my children are dead, am I still a mother?


Ah…
Pets don't count this time.


I'm a believer don't get that wrong.
I'm a believer of belief;
of the belief that everyone needs to believe in
something.
The need for faith is hardwired into our very hearts
and souls,
and I wonder if my children ever believed that they
would be able to experience a belief in something
other than me.


My faith is shattered and my desire to believe again
cracked.

There is no gold to repair it. These valleys of my
heart are deep and scarred.
Your Words can't fix this.
My words can't fix this.
They are a bandaid over a broken bone.


You may ask about my anger, because, yes, of
course I am angry.
Anger born from years of feeling like I am in a
Shakespearean nightmare.
Understand that my life shouldn't be me just
waiting on the next tragedy to occur.


The Poets are dead, and my rage lives on.
My children are dead, but my life rages on.
I'm done with this.
I've nothing more to say to You.
You aren't listening anyway.


Oh, wait! Sorry.
Forgive my forgetfulness.
It's been so long since I've done this.
I just remembered how it's supposed to end.


Amen.

# Disclaimer Part Two

Writing and compiling my poetry and prose into this book has been cathartic and healing. For over half my life I have had some diagnosis of anxiety and depression. In the last handful of years my husband and I lost all three of our children to stillbirth, premature birth, and miscarriage. This book contains writing from across my life from my first anxiety diagnosis over ten years ago to the autumn of 2025. This is my Blue Period.

www.ingramcontent.com/pod-product-compliance
Lightning Source LLC
Chambersburg PA
CBHW070652130626
46555CB00006B/2846